Feeding the Meter

Feeding the Meter

Poems by

Matthew Cory

Cover design by Shay Culligan
Cover image by Maël BALLAND on Unsplash
Author photo by Matthew Cory
Storm-cloud image by Ritam Baishya on Unsplash

ISBN: 979-8-90146-917-0
Library of Congress Control Number: 2026941442

Kelsay Books
502 South 1040 East, A-119
American Fork, Utah 84003
Kelsaybooks.com

To Mom
(Roberta "Bobbie" Jean Cory)

Acknowledgments

Writing poetry is the passion of the second half of my life. Without it, I would not be fulfilled as a person. Creating a poem and formulating a chapbook is no easy task. It takes dedication, determination, and a vulnerability to be critiqued. It also requires a support system of people filling distinct roles.

First and foremost, I would like to extend my greatest appreciation to my mother and father, who always encouraged me to follow my dreams, whatever they might be, and supported me whenever I left jobs or went in a different direction. I also want to express my deepest gratitude to my older brother Paul Cory, for assisting me when I began my writing journey by reading some of my early poems and offering constructive feedback. To his wife, Laura Haywood-Cory, thank you for taking the time to organize an earlier group of poems, so I could learn how that process works.

To Louise Rill, I am deeply grateful for your encouragement of my early writing, and for reading and listening to me recite those poems to you. To Jack McIver, I appreciate you reading my poems, offering critical feedback, and having confidence in my skills as a writer.

To my peers at Poetry Circle, thank you for reading and appreciating my poems. I want to send a special thanks to Claire, Leigh, Albert, Adam, and Tim for constructive feedback that helped shape some of the poems in this collection.

To my friends in my Charlotte Writers Club writing groups, thank you for your critical feedback on some of the poems found within these pages.

I am humbled by and sincerely appreciative of the following publications who placed some of the poems in this collection within their esteemed pages:

Blue Unicorn: "Retirement"

The Lyric: "Envy," "Burnside Bridge," "Tomorrow," "In the Blind," "Uninvited Guest," "Arlington," "Winterberry," "Failed Free Verse," "Yesterday," "Gratitude," "Nightcap"

The Orchards Poetry Journal: "For a Friend After the Death of Her Spouse," "Envy"

Westward Quarterly: "Shore Leave in the Mountains," "Summer Sonata," "Introspection"

Contents

Envy

There is no tide that wonders why
Its seashells litter beaches;
Fierce, focused waves don't sob or sigh
Or blight ears with sad speeches.

Perennials do not bemoan
Their withered blooms in winter;
Asleep in peace, no growl or groan
Is muttered in the ether.

The summer offers no lament
When autumn woos September;
Days do not sour with discontent
Or keep aglow an ember.

Forlorn, I sit in envy of
The tides, nature, and seasons,
Who never mourn or miss lost love
Nor dwell upon its reasons.

My Sorrow

My heart erodes with every drop
Of grief's incessant rain—
I'm told, in time, this storm will stop,
And Love will plant another crop
Of flowers, which will bloom atop
The ashes of my pain.

But months of mists have washed away
What fertile earth was there,
That should fresh seeds of love's bouquet
Ride winds and find this disarray,
They'll find a plot of sterile clay
And yield to its despair.

What Lies Beneath

The ocean paints its hue
From emerald green to blue
Where shallows meet the reef
And waves turn peace to grief.

Then nature sinks its woe
Two hundred feet below,
Its surface calm for miles—
A sea with doctored smiles.

A Walk with Charlotte Smith

Charlotte Smith (1749–1806) was an English poet whose work is considered a precursor to the Romantics.

I take a walk and make acquaintance with
Her kindred lyric spirit, passing through
A life bemired by melancholy's hue,
Where bliss exists in only dreams and myth.
We stroll along the cliffs of Brighton's bay,
Whose walls are beaten down by raging waves
As shards of earth are cast to ocean graves,
Beneath skies black as those that loom today.

We both look west, and see a firmament
Arrayed in sapphire hope and wonder why
Day's golden star illuminates the strands
Just miles away, while nature seems content
To keep us caged in shadow and deny
Our hearts the soothing light of distant lands.

Uninvited Guest

A cold gust slams my door,
Announcing your intent
To visit for a day or more—
I give you my consent.

I watch you pouring gin
Into an empty glass,
And note your grim, inverted grin,
As drinks go down en masse.

You walk in leaden shoes
And wear a draggled coat,
And scoff at smiles and pleasant hues,
Immune to antidote.

You don't provide a clue
To why you sulk and grieve,
And after days of gloom ensue,
You pack your bags and leave.

Relieved, my hands collect
The empty fifths of booze,
And cursing wind that left me wrecked,
I rue December's blues.

Death of a Sycamore

The sycamore sits still,
A skeleton in May.
Nests mourn a distant trill.

Shadows no longer spill
Across the verdant clay.
The sycamore sits still.

Once wren and whippoorwill
Spun leaves with heartfelt play.
Nests mourn a distant trill.

Now quietude is shrill
And lingers through the day.
The sycamore sits still.

Bark frays into a frill,
'Til gusts whisk it away.
Nests mourn a distant trill.

Mother Nature had her fill,
Then left it to decay.
The sycamore sits still.
Nests mourn a distant trill.

To Edwin Arlington Robinson

I’ve never met a night as dark as those
Bleak thoughts within the pages of your verse—
Despair and sadness wilt your flowers, and worse,
No resolution finds each stricken rose.
With every tome, your melancholy grows,
Your hardened stylus burdened by some curse
Which paints in dreary dress a universe
Where hope is carrion consumed by crows.

Yet hidden in your songs, between the lines,
A dogged breath pervades your doleful mood,
Enduring through the trials of gloom and death—
And as I close each book, this fortitude
Erodes my own despair, despite its breadth,
Until, at last, a shaft of sunlight shines.

Winterberry

I walk along a snow-draped field
Whose muted copses mourn
Abandoned nests they once concealed
Before their limbs were shorn.

Winds bellow autumn's last lament
As winter's gloomy gaze
Expresses kindred discontent
And welcomes my malaise.

The sun despairs behind the grey,
Resigned to its defeat,
And haunting footprints creep away,
Consumed by their deceit.

But by a broken gate, the fruit
Of winterberry blooms,
Its brilliant red hues resolute
Amid the drear that looms.

At once its charm begins to cleanse
My eyes and paint a scene
Beheld through optimism's lens,
Which prior, went unseen.

White palls of snow—now bridal dress,
Bleak silence—peaceful sleep.
The steady gusts that moaned distress
No longer seem to weep.

A smile repairs my sullen face,
My thoughts become serene—
I greet a new, auspicious place
Where hope is ever green.

For a Friend After the Death of Her Spouse

When breezes sway an empty chair
And kiss your trembling, sullen lips
While blossomed maple fingertips
Caress your locks of lemon hair;

When swirling gusts of April air
Wrap gentle arms around your hips
And dry each plaintive tear that drips
From curtained eyes with tender care—

Drink in the breaths that soothe despair
And savor them with tiny sips,
Then hoist the sails of love's lorn ships
And ride the wind—you'll find him there.

Tomorrow

When time's baton is passed between
The days, her form appears
And mocks me from afar—my mien
Bedecked with hopes and fears.

Outstretching her elusive hands,
She lures me with the keys
To speculation's blurry lands
But gives no guarantees.

As hours elapse, my bold pursuit
Diminishes our distance,
And yet I know the end is moot
No matter my persistence.

A breath away as midnight nears,
No closer do I get.
The clock strikes twelve, she disappears—
I haven't caught her yet.

Yesterday

Night's silver sentries never hear
Her footsteps when she leaves,
Nor watch her essence disappear
From ever changing eaves.
She steals away in quietude
Beyond the western sky
To join the growing multitude
Who sleep but cannot die.

What fingerprints she leaves behind
Assure her legacy
Lives in a new world redefined
For perpetuity,
Yet those who seek a second chance
Will learn it won't suffice
To surf old waves of circumstance
Without her sage advice.

She lingers in the minds of men
Inhaling joyous air
Or painful gales whose sad amen
Seems way too much to bear.
Yes, some will love, and some will rue
Her presence in their hearts,
But all will wear her residue
Long after she departs.

Mortality

The west's horizon, set aflame
At sunset, burns the dregs of day
As silver armies stake their claim
To skies subdued in twilight's fray.

Night's constellated legions fly
Their somber flag, its single hue
Reminding men that all things die
And time will win its war with you.

In the Blind

Inhaled, a deep and steady breath
Is measured, then released in kind,
As eyes look down the sights of death.
Inhaled, a deep and steady breath
Slows speeding heartbeats underneath
Calm camouflage—the shot's aligned.
Inhaled, a deep and steady breath
Is measured, half-released, resigned.

Arlington

Above a moonlit pall of snow,
Stand solemn sentries, row by row,
Whose earnest silence honors men
Who march beyond our earthen ken,
Amid the ranks of stars that glow.

Those laid to rest in beds below
Once loved and dreamed; some years ago
They gazed on sunset's red amen,
And hoped to greet the dawn again—
Yet fell to war's unyielding woe.

I walk the cemetery slow
And read the chiseled names aglow
In luna's light, and start to pen
A song for fallen servicemen
Who died for bards they'd never know.

Burnside Bridge

A placid stream strolls past a bed
Of lilacs tanning near the shore,
As cardinals and kestrels soar
Across the azure overhead.

A stout stone bridge of meager height
Takes tourists' feet across the creek
To emerald waves whose blades are sleek
And glisten in new morning light.

The peaceful trills and tranquil scene
Belie the savage, bloody fray
Men uniformed in blue and gray
Waged here one day on Union green.

I close my eyes and hear the guns
Drown out the songsters' civil songs,
And see the brook bestrewn with throngs
Of breathless brothers, dads, and sons.

A Soldier's Respite

As trooping billows fade to foam,
I savor salty air—
Thoughts once deployed are ordered home
To rest and seek repair.

The waves advance and I exhale
Until their march completes,
Then slowly, empty lungs inhale
While weary flows retreat.

Beyond the dunes, peace bleeds to fray
And all my swords unsheathe,
But here, the strand disarms dismay
And soothes each breath I breathe.

Gratitude

Dawn emerges, devoid of gold,
Yet still the bluebirds strain
As if the sky shone sevenfold
To light the day's terrain.

The sparrows carol, flit, and play,
The robins sing along—
Unfazed by morning's gloomy grey,
Compelled to belt their song.

Perhaps there is some latent bliss
Within each songster's breast,
Saved treasure for a day like this—
To deem it heaven blessed.

Or maybe their elation springs
From gratitude, aware
All daybreaks are God-given things
That merit joyous air.

Shore Leave in the Mountains

Earthen waves crash into vales
Beneath a sea-foam sky
As daytime's star hoists fuchsia sails
And bids its quay goodbye.

My harbor calm, my crew at rest,
I scan the loamy deep,
Relaxed while silver flecks the west
And placid shallows sleep.

Summer Sonata

Atop a stage of elms and oaks,
Trimmed in August's emerald cloaks,
A forest-filling symphony
Of birdsong echoes tree to tree.

Wrens and sparrows play their flutes
While pausing from their winged pursuits,
Then cardinals sound clarinets
To join the warbling wind quartets.

Mourning doves coo cello notes
And barred owl bassists rouse their throats
To hoot a baseline's steady thrum
As red-bellied woodpeckers drum.

The wood's sonata halts my walk—
I picture Chopin, Brahms and Bach
Composing 'neath the firmament,
Inspired by nature's instruments.

To a Carolina Wren

Inspired by dawn, your lays provide
The soundtrack for the day
In every vale and mountain side,
Beneath skies blue or grey.

The richness of your morning song
Makes other strains seem plain,
And stirs my head to nod along
When I traipse field or lane.

Sweet balladeer, why hide from sight
Within some brushy sty,
And never see your trills delight
The ears of passers-by?

I yearn to watch you standing proud
Atop a twiggy stage,
More confident than lines allowed
To grace a poet's page.

But as my footsteps venture near,
Before I catch a look,
You dart away, then disappear
To seek a safer nook.

Oh, timidest of all the birds!
You need not fear or curse
The blissful bard that chases words
To capture you in verse!

At Walden Pond

We sit across from one another's gaze,
Discussing the importance of Thoreau
And whether self-sufficiency can grow
Philosophies deserving of our praise.
You argue morals borne of lonely days,
Away from interaction's back and forth,
Are forged in paltry candlelight—their worth
Diminished by those produced in parley's blaze.

But when I ask if you have ever been
Alone in nature, meek beneath the sun,
Removed from shopworn sentiments of men
Whose bubbles don't enlighten anyone,
You scoff, then stand and grab your book and pen,
And leave me a majority of one.

Discretion

We met again by happenstance
Amid mid-summer's haze,
Regret for unexplored romance
Affixed upon our gaze.
I asked about her family—
She shared a bleak review,
Detailing the disharmony
Her marriage suffered through.

Attentive to the boundaries
A wife must always keep,
I offered her my hand to squeeze
When she began to weep.
She grasped it for a little while
Until time eased her cries,
Then flashed a faint, but fervent smile
And thanked me with her eyes.

We lingered there a moment more
Beneath noon's golden glare,
But soon the weight of vows she swore
Was far too much to bear.
Without a word, resigned to cope
With months of new remorse,
We parted ways, eschewing hope
To let life take its course.

Nightcap

From far across the bar, she steals my gaze,
Arrays her visage with a subtle smile
And looks into my hazel eyes awhile,
Recalling fervent nights that soothed malaise.
She toasts me with a wink, I nod and raise
My brow, and resurrected is the guile
We shared—until she chose to reconcile
And honor vows devoid of ardent days.

And there beside her sits the distant groom
Who never pays her any heed, and I
Walk past them slow, inhaling her perfume,
And catch one final glance flung from her eye.
In secret, we acknowledge thoughts that loom,
And then she turns and whispers him a lie.

The Regular

When any stranger met him, they would think
His smile was filled with more than common grace,
For zeal and zest were fixtures on his face,
And wreathed in stogie smoke, he'd fling a wink.
He always offered visitors a drink,
Relating tales besotted fools embrace
As raucous laughter overtook the place,
Then he would pay the tab without a blink.

And so, it was to most a grim surprise
He hung himself last night, his door ajar
For all to see, while friends who knew his guise
And wishes, each sat at the local bar,
Set alight an extravagant cigar,
Caroused and reminisced his blissful lies.

Sophie

When Carrie said *I love you,*
She could not meet my gaze,
And when her brown eyes tried to,
Her lips forsook the phrase.

Melinda often wrote it
When distance intervened,
But struggled to emote it
Each time we reconvened.

Not once has Sophie spoken
Or typed those words to me,
And yet my heart’s unbroken,
Secure with what I see—

Her eyes declare a passion
Oblivious to time,
A stare so deep, to ration
Its hold would be a crime.

Lesser Poet

I am a mockingbird, my paltry tunes
Are feeble covers of more dulcet trills
From bluebirds, chickadees, and whippoorwills
Whose strains have hailed the dawns and afternoons
For centuries, inspiring pens at rest
To wake and praise their melodies in lines
Imbued with reverence. Such artful shrines
Will never laud one note flung from my breast.

And though my meager lays may fail to climb
Olympian heights, perhaps a passer-by
Will hear my imitations and depart
Recalling songs of songsters more sublime,
Then head to haunts nearby, where perched on high,
The masters rapture ears with blissful art.

Introspection

I savor silence in its many forms—
A house asleep as morning steals the night,
The quietude of dawning beams of light
Soon after skies dispose of summer storms,
The hush of autumn's multicolored swarms
Meandering through air in winsome flight,
The peaceful orbit of earth's satellite,
And muted landscapes winter snow transforms.

These soundless moments steer my thoughts within,
Beneath my shallow, repetitious breath,
Into the crevices of heart and soul,
Where new epiphanies forge thicker skin
And fresh perspectives sorting life and death,
Amending once half-truths to make them whole.

Retirement

I stand on edge inside of labor's keep,
Arrayed in saving's armor, raise the gate,
And glimpse the landscape of tomorrow's fate,
Unsure if there are harvests I can reap.
The road is long, the hills ahead are steep,
Which cause the surest men to hesitate,
But somewhere there awaits a new estate
Where I can tend to different flocks of sheep.

I lift my shield of faith and sword of trust
To fight conviction's everlasting foe,
And parrying, I launch one final thrust,
Dispatching fear which falls into the snow.
I step outside the walls, and let a gust
Determine the direction I should go.

Failed Free Verse

I tried to pen this poem free
From iambs, yet the words
Keep beat in meter, steadily
As flitting wings of birds.

No rhymes were meant to end these lines,
But neither can a throng
Of wrens not sing when sunlight shines,
Nor I not write a song.

About the Author

Matthew Cory is a retired tennis teaching professional in Matthews, NC. He spends his days writing and taking care of his German Shepherd, Greta. His poems have been featured in *The Lyric, Blue Unicorn, Westward Quarterly,* and *The Orchards Poetry Journal.* He counts Thomas Hardy, Edward Arlington Robinson, Edna St. Vincent Millay, and Henry Wadsworth Longfellow among his poetic inspirations.

www.ingramcontent.com/pod-product-compliance
Lightning Source LLC
LaVergne TN
LVHW050611100826
845148LV00015B/3224

* 9 7 9 8 9 0 1 4 6 9 1 7 0 *